Valery Berthoud

An Inquiry on Modal Metaphysical Puzzling Possible Worlds

Anchor Academic
Publishing

Berthoud, Valery: An Inquiry on Modal Metaphysical Puzzling Possible Worlds,
Hamburg, Anchor Academic Publishing 2017

Buch-ISBN: 978-3-96067-194-7
PDF-eBook-ISBN: 978-3-96067-694-2
Druck/Herstellung: Anchor Academic Publishing, Hamburg, 2017
Covermotiv: © pixabay.de

Bibliografische Information der Deutschen Nationalbibliothek:
Die Deutsche Nationalbibliothek verzeichnet diese Publikation in der Deutschen
Nationalbibliografie; detaillierte bibliografische Daten sind im Internet über
http://dnb.d-nb.de abrufbar.

Bibliographical Information of the German National Library:
The German National Library lists this publication in the German National Bibliography.
Detailed bibliographic data can be found at: http://dnb.d-nb.de

© Anchor Academic Publishing, Imprint der Diplomica Verlag GmbH
Hermannstal 119k, 22119 Hamburg
http://www.diplomica-verlag.de, Hamburg 2017
Printed in Germany

Abstract

The concept of possible worlds is useful because it defines the four modalities – possibility, necessity, contingency, and impossibility – but a challenge lies in defining it. The polemical hypothesis from David Lewis ("genuine modal realism" as it is called) succeeds in it. Lewis' modal realism stirred controversy because he maintains that a plurality of worlds exists. Some philosophers suggest that the Lewisian view is a violation to the law of parsimony, also known as Ockham's Razor – "don't multiply entities beyond necessity" (Spade and Panaccio 2015). While avoiding a circular definition, Lewis constructs an inflated ontology. Is it worth it, and if we do not want to assume too many Lewisian worlds, what alternatives remain? Actualist modal realism and modal antirealism are the most relevant alternatives because modal abstentionism simply will not progress in this direction. This thesis evaluates theories of possible worlds.

Acknowledgements

For his proofreading and all the work he has done to help me through the learning and writing process of this bachelor thesis, I would like to offer my special thanks to Jonathan Mai.

Many thanks to all the people who discussed ideas with me, who provided me with very valuable inspiration and useful comments.

Foremost, I am much obliged to my family for their support and guidance.

Contents

List of Figures

List of Symbols

☐   Necessity (necessarily)

Δ   Possible worlds, a W with a subscript numeral is also used instead of uppercase Greek letters

◇   Possibility (possibly)

≡   Material equivalence, (if and only if; iff)

∃   Existential quantification (there exists)

∀   Universal quantification (for all; for any; for each)

¬   Negation (not), $\neg A$ is true only if A is false

∨   Inclusive disjunction (or)

φ   Lowercase Greek letters are used for formulae

∴   Therefore sign

→   Material conditional (implies; if A then B)

∧   Conjunction (and)

P Uppercase Roman letters are used for propositions

Part I

Background

Introduction

"Do you come to a philosopher as to a cunning man, to learn something by magic or witchcraft, beyond what can be known by common prudence and discretion?"

— David Hume (1793)

The title of this bachelor thesis, "An Inquiry on Modal, Metaphysical, Puzzling Possible Worlds", includes four adjectives that qualify the noun *worlds*: possible, puzzling, metaphysical, and modal. *Possible* and *worlds* coalesce into the concept of possible worlds, and the remaining three adjectives qualify it. *Puzzling* indicates the enigma that is the concept of possible worlds, and *metaphysical* relates possible worlds to things treated in the framework of metaphysics.[1] Finally, *modal* characterises possible worlds by asserting or denying possibility, impossibility, contingency, or necessity. This thesis is explanatory, and the debate begins by defining possible worlds, a concept that contemporary philosophers use often.

I deal with a metaphysical question. My position regarding metaphysical questions is that we can seek answers, since such questions are part of a branch of philosophy. Therefore, my method is to seek clarification of the concepts as it is usual in philosophy.

---

[1] Metaphysics is a branch of philosophy that examines the nature of reality and investigates the fundamental nature of being and the world; it answers what there is and what it is like.

1

Modalities

This chapter offers a broad perspective on modalities, and I begin by defining modality and explaining types of them: logical, metaphysical, nomological, epistemic, doxastic, deontic, and temporal.[2] I then define the four modalities: possibility, contingency, necessity, and impossibility. Modality refers to the way things might have been; if a possibility is asserted, impossibility is disqualified.

(1) Life is possible.

When stating that (1) impossibility is disqualified, it is impossible that life is not possible, and we do not have to prove it. The four modalities interrelate; possibility requires contingency or necessity, but it cannot be both, inasmuch as contingency contradicts necessity and vice versa. The difference lies in whether it need not be or it must be. Contingency and necessity both require possibility, and both disqualify impossibility. Thus, impossibility disqualifies possibility, contingency, and necessity (cf. Divers 2002, pp. 3-4). Statements that suggest what must be, cannot be, may be, or need not be are called modal statements, of which there are multiple types. Modal statements appear to be true.

---

[2]I do this because it is easier to understand the nature of possible worlds if they are involved with modal discourse.

(2) Possible worlds exist.

Depending on the understanding of (2), possible worlds exist either in a logical, metaphysical, or physical space. Shown in figure 1.1 (Vaidya 2015),

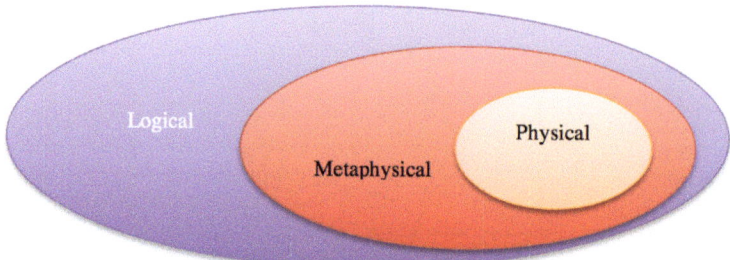

Figure 1.1: Relation between modalities

logical modality is the most inclusive, and logical modality is fixed by the laws of logic. One proposition must be true and the other false, and if they are contradictory propositions, this is the law of the excluded middle, which brings us to the law of non-contradiction: there is no proposition such that both it and its negation are true. Apart from logical modality, other types can be classified, of which metaphysical modality is one, fixed by the laws of metaphysics (e.g., the nature and identity conditions of things). Metaphysical modality includes everything that might have existed. Something is metaphysically necessary if it is determined by the laws of metaphysics, and it is possible if compatible with the laws of metaphysics.[3] The origin and constitution of something are the type of properties that are thought to be essential. I cannot lose the property of being human; this property is metaphysically necessary. Magic is metaphysically possible. An example is growing larger or smaller after eating cake like Alice in Wonderland. This is not physically possible. Nomological modality is fixed by the laws of

[3]Some suggest no disparity between logical and metaphysical spaces, but it is difficult to think of metaphysical modalities that are not concordant with logical modalities.

4

physical reality; the laws of nature have to allow it. Something is nomologically necessary if it is determined by the laws of nature, and it is possible if compatible with the laws of nature. It is nomologically necessary that an isolated system's entropy always increases over time, and it is nomologically possible to jump five meters (e.g., on the moon) (cf. Priest 2008, pp. 46-47). Another type is deontic modality, determined by what satisfies a norm or rule. Something is deontically necessary if it is required by the laws of morality, and deontically possible if permitted. Temporal modality is fixed by time; something is temporally necessary if it is true at all times, and temporally possible if true sometimes (cf. ibid., pp. 46-47). Another type of modality is epistemic. Facts that can be known or believed (e.g., evidence) are epistemic modal notions. Epistemic modality is fixed by what is known. If something is known to be true, it is epistemically necessary, and epistemically possible if it might be true. Doxastic modality is fixed by what is believed. If something is believed true, it is doxastically necessary, and doxastically possible if it could be believed. A debate exists regarding whether epistemic modalities are different from metaphysical ones (cf. Kment 2012). Dualists argue for a fundamental distinction between epistemic and metaphysical modalities, but monists for only a single type of modality (cf. ibid.) I argue that it is possible to distinguish a metaphysical notion of necessity from an epistemic one. Regardless of whether one is a dualist or monist, it is possible to differentiate them and distinguish both epistemic and metaphysical reasons to seek a reduction of the definition of modality. Asking "Why seek such a reduction?" is like asking why philosophers avoid circular reasoning. The reasons have to do with connections among modality, epistemology, and metaphysics. Modality is important to philosophy because it connects with epistemology and metaphysics, and these connections are influential in analytic philosophy. Epistemology of the modal requires reductionism to define modal notions in terms that do not include modal notions and can therefore be the epistemology of the modal secured. A metaphysical reason for seeking reduction is to begin an ontology with primitive notions that are non-modal (cf. Sider 2003, p. 5).

1.1 Possibility

There are two ways of expressing possibilities: *possible for* is a qualifiable possibility, and *possible that* is a variable possibility (cf. Girle 2009, pp. 140-141). The first phrase can be qualified using words such as logically, metaphysically, and physically. For example:

(3) It is physically possible for light to travel at 299,792,458 m/s.

The second phrase can vary using terms such as quite and definite:

(4) It is definitely not possible for time to stop.

There is a connection between (3) and (4).

(5) If it is impossible to travel at the speed of light, then it is impossible for time to stop.

The reverse does not hold:

(6) If it is impossible for time to stop, then it is impossible to travel at the speed of light.

Shown in 1.1, if something is possible, it depends on the considered type of modality.

(7) I could have done better.

Sentence (7) expresses possibility (i.e., can, might, could). We can imagine what would have happened were the course of things different. Imagine a painter choosing the colour blue instead of orange; the resulting painting is different. What if my parents had not met and I had not been born? I would not be here writing this thesis because existence is contingent.

1.2 Contingency

A contingent proposition might or might not happen; the event could occur, but is unnecessary. Logical contingency means something that is neither logically necessary nor impossible. Maybe, maybe not, might have been, might not have been and could have been otherwise – these are ways of expressing contingency (cf. Girle 2009, p. 3). In Figure 1.2, Ohrstrom and Hasle (2015) illustrate an idea from Saul Kripke, concerning branching time, in which Kripke considers the present as a point of Rank 1, the next possible event as point of Rank 2, etc.

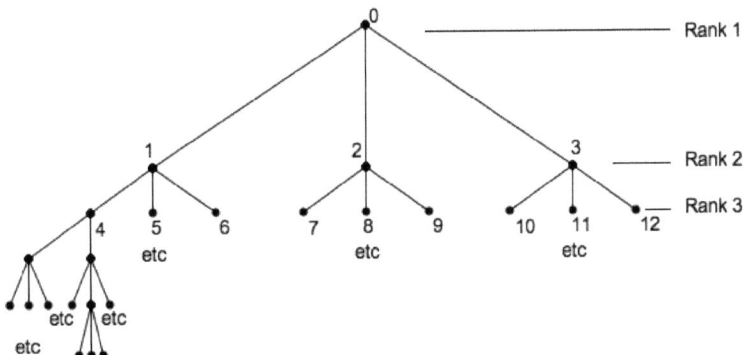

Figure 1.2: Tree structure of possible futures

(8) It might rain today.

For example, if someone says (8) at point 0, point 1 could be sunny, point 2 cloudy, and point 3 thunderstorm. Plans depend on contingent weather, and we depend on contingent events because the future is uncertain. This uncertainty will always change plans.

(9) If it rains, the picnic will be cancelled.

7

The picnic depends on something that is neither necessarily true nor false. A proposition is contingent if its contrary does not imply a contradiction. When speaking, we make statements about the future, and most are contingent.

(10) In 1999, a great King of terror will come from the sky.

When Nostradamus wrote (10), it was neither true nor false because the year 1999 did not exist. Future contingents are neither true nor false (cf. Priest 2008, p. 132).

1.3 Necessity

Our lives are full of decisions, leading to endless possibilities, but despite so many possibilities, necessity expresses that something could not be otherwise. Necessity (i.e., must and has to be) is another case of modality. Something necessary is understood as an inevitable consequence. There is a discussion about whether some things could have been otherwise. Many things appear metaphysically possible, but more disagreement exists regarding whether metaphysical principles are necessary. Some philosophers argue that metaphysical principles are merely contingent.[4] An important question is whether anything is necessary – does a nomological necessity exist? Are the laws of nature necessary? There is also an ongoing debate on whether necessity must associate with the laws of nature, and some examples suggest doubt. What about mathematical truths?

---

[4]For example, Ross Cameron argues that metaphysical principles are contingent because were they necessary, it would lead to an unwarranted universalism (cf. Cameron 2007, p. 99).

1.4 Impossibility

Something impossible cannot be done and cannot happen, and many agree that something that violates the natural laws is impossible. Lewis argues that what usually counts as nomologically impossible is possible, "so the laws are not sacred" (Lewis 1973, p. 567). Another definition of impossibility contradicts the laws of classical logic, like the law of non-contradiction. Consensus suggests that contradictions are impossible unless the law of non-contradiction is invalid, as in the position of dialethism. Dialethists defend the view that some contradictions are true; hence, for them, logical laws are not sacred. Graham Priest suggests no problem with discriminations concerning impossibility (cf. Priest 2008, p. 15).

2

Modal Logic

I turn to modal logic in this chapter, examining its background and development, and then introduce modal logic, assessing axioms and common possible worlds semantics. Modal logic was created at the same time as logic. Aristotle provided partial analysis of problems raised by modality, investigating the validity of modal syllogisms. The history of modal logic traces to Megarian logicians.[5] Medieval logic books include principles of modal syllogism, which indicates that modal logic was discussed during the Middle Ages. The empiricist tradition embraces skepticism regarding modalities. The system B was formulated by Kurt Gödel, who was first to propose that the syntactical notion of provability – especially as understood by Luitzen Brouwer, after whom the system was named – can be represented by the modal notion of necessity (cf. Cocchiarella and Freund 2008, p. 37). Clarence Lewis initiated modal logic during the modern period; he defined a logic of conditionals that do not have the necessity signs. At that time, Paul Carnap worked out the Leibnizian idea that necessary truth is truth across all possible worlds. During the first half of the century, logicians failed to identify models for modal systems, and were incapable of providing complete proofs of the systems. The subject was criticised by

---

[5]Euclid of Megara founded the Megarian school, and Philo the Dialectician was its most prominent exponent.

Willard Quine, whose work made it unpopular (cf. Priest 2008, p. 33). The situation changed when Kripke invented relational semantics. The 19-year-old undergraduate achieved some of the first complete theorems in modal logic, which were constructed from a weak system called K (after Kripke). During the 1960s, many other logicians such as Richard Montague, Stig Kanger, and Kaarlo Hintikka continued to elaborate on Leibnizian idea, and developed what we know today as modal logic (cf. Loux 1979, pp. 16-20).

2.1 What is Modal Logic?

Logic investigates the principles of correct reasoning and the difference between valid and invalid arguments – the principles of inferential relations. Modal logic is a type of formal logic concerned with modalities, studying reasoning that involves use of modal expressions. The term *modal logic* covers much logics with similar rules and diversity of symbols. In addition to conjunctions ($\wedge$), disjunctions ($\vee$), conditionals ($\rightarrow$), and negations ($\neg$), modal logic deals with possibilities and necessities. Beyond the usual Boolean operators of classical logic, modal logic contains modal operators $\Diamond$ and $\Box$, the primitive symbols of possibility and necessity (cf. Garson 2016).

$\Diamond P$ is translated as *P might be true, it is possible that P,* or *possibly P.*

$\Box P$ is translated as *P must be true, it is necessary that P,* or *necessarily P.*

$\Diamond P \wedge \Diamond \neg P$ is translated as *P is contingent.*

$\Box P \vee \Box \neg P$ is translated as *P is analytic* (cf. Girle 2009, p. 9).

11

A differentiation exists between *extension* and *intension*. The extension of a term is the thing to which it refers, and the extension of a predicate is the set of things to which it refers. The intension of a term is determined by its possible extensions. A logic is extensional if the truth value of any sentence is determined by the extensions of the terms and predicates. Hence, the principle of substitutivity *salva veritate* applies in extensional logic, meaning that if two terms have the same extension, either can be substituted for the other. In contrast, substitutivity does not apply in intensional logics (cf. Menzel 2016).

(11) All of Claude's dogs are mammals ($\forall x (Dx \to Mx)$).

(12) All of Claude's pets are mammals ($\forall x (Px \to Mx)$).

We can substitute *dogs* in (11) for *pets* in (12) *salva veritae*. Suppose that all of Claude's pets are three dogs. Since (11) and (12) are true, substitutivity holds.

(13) Necessarily, all of Claude's dogs are mammals ($\Box \forall x (Dx \to Mx)$).

(14) Necessarily, all of Claude's pets are mammals ($\Box \forall x (Px \to Mx)$).

For modal statements such as (13) and (14), however, substitution fails and (14) is false since Claude could have birds, reptiles, or other non-mammalian pets (cf. ibid.) In classical logic,[6] validity can be defined using truth tables, but they cannot provide validity in modal logics because there are no truth tables for modal expressions. Modal logic is intensional, without a semantic theory that systematises modal truth. Modal statements express a way things might have been. Our world is not that way, and therefore we cannot find any extension. If I talk about the possible existence of a perpetual motion machine, nothing in our world covers that term.

---

[6]This type of logic is concerned with the study of whether propositions are true or false.

De Dicto and De re

In this subsection, I discuss the *de dicto* - *de re* distinction. *De dicto* and *de re* are phrases used to mark an important distinction, well known in philosophy of language and metaphysics. The literal translation of *de dicto* is "about what is said", and "*de re*" translates as "about the thing". There is a grammatical contrast between *de re* and *de dicto* sentences. In *de re* sentences, a variable in the scope of the modal operator is bound to a quantifier outside the scope, whereas in *de dicto* sentences, no quantification occurs (cf. Sider 2003, p. 3). Consequently, there is a difference between (15) and (16):

(15) Ludwig believes that Athena is the goddess of wisdom.

(16) Athena was venerated because of her wisdom.

Sentence (15) is read *de dicto* ("Ludwig believes that possibly Athena is the goddess of wisdom"). Sentence (16) is *de re*. From a formal perspective, the difference is clear. A *de re* modality is viewed as if the scope[7] of the modal operator contains a free occurrence of an individual variable. Otherwise, if the scope of the modal operator contains no free occurrence of an individual variable, it expresses a modality *de dicto*. The definition of both phrases sets out from the scope. Consider the sentences:

(17) Necessarily, the number of major deities of the Greek pantheon is even.

(18) The number of major deities of the Greek pantheon is such that it is necessarily even.

With respect to (17), it is *de dicto*, and translates to:[8]

---

[7] *Scope* indicates on what the □ operates.

[8] In the *de re* translation, the bracketed lambda expresses the property of being necessarily even. Iota denotes the number of the major deities. The whole formula says that the number has the property.

$$\Box(\lambda x.\ Ex)(\iota z.\ Nz)$$

(18) is a *de re* modality, and translates to:

$$(\lambda x.\ \Box Ex)(\iota z.\ Nz)$$

There might have been thirteen Olympias instead of twelve, and therefore (17) is untrue because it claims that the number of Olympians is even in all possible worlds. However, (18) claims only that the number twelve is necessarily even. If an object has a *de re* modality, then the modality expresses that the object has the property essentially[9] or accidentally[10] (cf. Menzel 2016). Discussed in Chapter One, essentialism[11] is found in the work of Aristotle. Thomas Aquinas agrees with Aristotle (cf. Plantinga 1969, p. 236), stating that *de re* necessities are true only when the essence is the focus.

(19) Johann is necessarily meditating.

As an illustration, (19) is false if taken *de re* but true if taken *de dicto*. It is necessarily true that Johann is meditating; this is the *de dicto* interpretation of (19). The *de re* reading understands that Johann has the property of meditating essentially, but this seems false,[12] since Johann could stop meditating and still be him. Many philosophers are against essentialism, but at this point, we have touched on an area that is no longer formal logic, but metaphysical.

---

[9]If z has a property P in every possible world in which z exists, z has the P essentially.
[10]If z has a property P in some world (but not all worlds), z has P accidentally.
[11]A philosophical position, according to which it is useful to distinguish what is necessarily true regarding some objects.
[12]One question is whether it is possible to eliminate all *de re* modalities in favor of modality *de dicto*. According to George Hughes and Max Cresswell, formal elimination is very difficult. Alan White conversely maintains that the distinction is based on the incorrect assumption that what is qualified when the whole is qualified is a proposition (i.e., about what is said). If White is correct, the *de dicto* - *de re* debate is vacuous (cf. Girle 2009, pp. 148-149).

2.2 Possible Worlds Semantics

Gottfried Leibniz argues that the real world is one of an infinite number of all possible worlds existing in the mind of God. His view attracted the attention of contemporary philosophers, and helped develop possible worlds semantics (cf. Stalnaker 1976, pp. 65-66). Leibniz defines the modalities as (cf. Look 2013):

⋆ Possibility: A proposition is possible iff it is true in some possible world.

⋆ Contingency: A proposition is contingently true iff it is true in this world and false in another.

⋆ Necessity: A proposition is necessarily true iff it is true in every possible world.

⋆ Impossibility: A proposition is impossible iff it is not true in any possible world.

Possible worlds express modal statements. Carnap initiated possible worlds semantics, and Leibniz' biconditionals give substance to alternative extensions and domains of quantification. This conception of possible worlds semantics is an essential element of Kripke's relational semantics for modal logic. The possible worlds proposed by Kripke for modal propositional logics is an ordered triple: $<W, R, \Vdash>$. W is a non-empty set, members of W are possible worlds, and R is a binary relation with W. $\Vdash$ is a relationship between possible worlds and additional variables (i.e., atomic formulae) that assigns a truth value (cf. Priest 2008, p. 21). Semantics for quantified modal logics require only an additional function that assigns a set to each member of W. In possible worlds semantics, a set Δ of possible worlds is needed. Valuations give a truth value to each formula for each possible world, and by introducing possible worlds, we can define semantics for

15

modal logics. System K is characterised by the models, whose relationship R is unrestricted. This class contains the models in which the following axiom is valid.

$$\Box\,(\varphi \rightarrow \psi) \rightarrow (\Box\,\varphi \rightarrow \Box\,\psi)$$

K is too weak and cannot provide an adequate account of necessity, but by adding axioms to the basic system K, we get a new system (cf. Garson 2016). System M was first described by Robert Feys, who suggests that whatever is necessary is the case, so the following axiom is provable:

$$\Box\,\varphi \rightarrow \varphi$$

System $S4$ adds the following to system M:

$$\Box\,\varphi \rightarrow \Box\,\Box\,\varphi$$

and system $S5$ adds the following to system M:

$$\Box\,\varphi \rightarrow \Box\,\Diamond\,\varphi$$

Systems $S4$ and $S5$ were described by C. Lewis and Cooper Langford (cf. Cocchiarella and Freund 2008, p. 28). Consider the following:

$$\varphi \rightarrow \Box\,\Diamond\,\varphi$$
$$\frac{\Box\,\varphi \rightarrow \Box\,\Box\,\varphi}{\Diamond\,\varphi \rightarrow \Box\,\Diamond\,\varphi}$$

The last axiom can be deduced from the first ones. If the possibility and necessity signs are interpreted as restricted quantifiers over a set of entities called possible worlds, the axioms "turn out to correspond to simple conditions on the relation whereby the box and diamond are restricted" (Lewis 1986, pp. 17-18). There are equivalences between $\Diamond$ and $\Box$ just as in predicate logic[13] with $\exists$ and $\forall$ (cf. Girle 2009, pp. 3-7). The modal negation equivalences are:

---

[13]In classical predicate logic, formulae that contain quantifiable individual variables can be formed.

(i) $\neg \Diamond S \equiv \Box \neg S$

(ii) $\Diamond \neg S \equiv \neg \Box S$

(iii) $\Box S \equiv \neg \Diamond \neg S$

(iv) $\Diamond S \equiv \neg \Box \neg S$

(20) The sun is shining.

Therefore, the logical equivalences of (20) are translated as:

  (i) It is impossible that the sun is shining iff it is necessary that the sun is not shining.

  (ii) It is possible that the sun is not shining iff it is unnecessary that the sun is shining.

  (iii) The sun must be shining iff it is impossible that the sun is not shining.

  (iv) The sun might be shining iff it is unnecessary that the sun is not shining.

Many expressions of natural language can be translated into modal logic, but it is important to be careful when translating the natural language. This is so with conditionals. The next argument shows that the necessity sign qualifies and operates on the conditionals.

(21) If I think about possible worlds, then possible worlds are.

If we let

  $A = $ I think

  $B = $ I am

the conditional is translated correctly as $\Box(A \to B)$ and incorrectly to $(A \to \Box B)$ since the implication is necessarily true, but the consequence is not. If we let

17

C = I think about possible worlds

D = Possible worlds are

then we translate to:

$$\Box(A \to B)$$
$$\Box(B \to C)$$
$$\Box(C \to D)$$
$$\neg \Diamond D$$
$$\overline{\therefore \neg \Diamond A}$$

In other words, if possible worlds cannot be, then I cannot think. The conclusion is not necessarily true, but the premises necessarily imply the conclusion (cf. Girle 2009, pp. 4-7). It is difficult to add classical quantifiers to the principles of modal logic. Similarly, Quine argues that it is incoherent to quantify into modal contexts because the intersubstitutivity principle fails and extensionality is lost (cf. Ramírez 2015, p. 29). Quine was skeptical about modal metaphysics, but he was a pragmatist, and from his viewpoint, if a theory is useful, it is worth believing. Kripke shows with his semantics and theory of rigid designators that quantifying into modal contexts is not complicated, assuming possible worlds is a primitive notion (cf. ibid., p. 34). Lewis, Quine's best student, does not subscribe to Kripke's relational semantics because it is ambiguous and has "devious semantic rules that work different ways in different cases" (Lewis 1986, p. 12). x must satisfy a formula in *absentia*, and in the case of different worlds, we get different cases (e.g., "x exists", "x is human", and "x is human and x does not exist" are different cases). If x is "essentially human", we mean "necessarily such that it is human if it exists", but we do not mean only "necessarily human" (Ibid., p. 12). Lewis proposes a theory that offers solutions to the problems that Quine raises. He proposes the thesis that our world is a plurality of worlds, and therefore he can quantify into modal contexts and regain extensionality using counterpart theory. With every gain there is a loss, and with every loss a gain. Lewis' theory gains simplification, unification, and explanatory power from philosophy, and most philosophers argue that the loss is common sense (cf. Ramírez 2015, p. 78). The problem is how to systematise modalities most suitably. Quine is an eliminativist; he denies modality. Kripke is a primitivist since modality remains unanalysed. Lewis is a modal reductionist.

We can understand possibility if modality is not the foundation stone. Modality, if it exists, is given by the underlying fact that we have to analyze modality. The problem is understanding what is modal knowledge. Facts about modality are different from facts about how our world is. It is not clear how it is that we have access to possibilities that are not actual. The implementation of the reduction program can solve the problem of modal knowledge. If we reduce modality to concepts that are non-modal, we can have access to knowledge that is absolutely normal, because then modal knowledge consists in a specific access to non-modal. According to Ockham's Razor, the best theory is the one with the fewest assumptions. Reduction should be done whenever possible, because a theory should be as simple as possible. Therefore, if we can reduce an entity, we should reduce it. This principle is a method for finding solutions to problems, because certain requirements are met, like a theory being simple. The simpler the theory is, the better. Then, we should reduce when it is possible to reduce.

Part II

What Are Possible Worlds?

3

Theories of Possible Worlds

Modal logics include set Δ of possible worlds. In possible worlds semantics, predication becomes world relative when objects exemplify properties with respect to worlds. Kripke restricts quantifiers so that they do not range over possible objects with an extension. The problem is that he does not define *possible world*, which was taken as primitive in metalanguage (cf. Zalta 2011, pp. 16-17). Leibniz' ontology gives content to possible worlds semantics insofar as his intuitive formulations to define modalities created the concept of possible worlds. When the concept began to be used, it showed heuristic power. If analyses of modal concepts in terms of possible worlds are heuristic, the concept of possible worlds must still be explained and justified (cf. Stalnaker 1976, p. 66). This chapter addresses this possible-world-discussion, consisting of what are possible worlds and whether they are concrete or abstract. I consider deeply the possible-world-discussion and address the question of what possible worlds are, and various perspectives regarding their definition. The purpose is to provide insights into disparate theories of possible worlds using an interpretative method to explain, compare, and assess them. First, I consider modal realism generally, distinguishing modal abstentionism, antirealism, and realism. Abstentionism is not wanting to talk about possible worlds. Antirealism persists in the use of possible worlds, but does not believe in them. And modal realism suggests that possible world sentences are capable of being true or false, for example, genuine modal realism; Lewis, one of its exponents, argues that possible worlds are just like this world, and hence a genuine modal realist claims that there exist countless other worlds like ours. Maybe this is too much to accept, but the actualist modal realist view suggests that the only world of which we are a part is concrete, and possible worlds are abstract. According to this position, the actual world is different from the concrete totality of things since possible worlds are abstract. I present four strategies of actualist modal realism: Plantingan, combinatorialism, nature, and book. I include neo-Meinongianism because we can make sense of impossible worlds. Although use of the notion of possible worlds was pioneered years later *inter alios* by Kripke, the Meinongian view of non-actual objects is one position to take. At the conclusion of the chapter, I discuss hybrid modal realism, which is the position I favour.

Abstentionism

Abstentionism is the refusal to participate in a discussion (i.e., to hold oneself back voluntarily from something regarded as improper). An abstentionist in this frame of philosophy, as the word suggests, abstains from possible-world-talk and possible-world-discussion. This frame is not useful, though the advantage is that no interpretations must be provided since no applications are needed (cf. Divers 2002, p. 19). Fortunately, it is an unpopular position since modal abstentionists hold back from expressing their views rather than contributing to the discussion. Philosophers should express their opinions if they have them, and abstentionists have opinions on possible worlds. The counterargument is that philosophical problems do not require commitment to possible worlds, and therefore abstentionists have the right to be silent and think that possible-world-talk is nonsense.[14]

Antirealism

I specify the approach of antirealism before focusing on the debate among realists. Antirealism is underdeveloped in comparison to realist views; no attempt has been made to assess the capacity of any antirealistic interpretation of possible worlds to deliver associated applications of possible worlds. The defenders of antirealism still deny a plurality of worlds. The difference with abstentionism is that antirealism persists in using possible worlds simply because they are helpful. Antirealism uses other strategies, the first of which is that possible world sentences (*it is possible that P iff there is some world Δ, in which it is the case that P*) cannot be true or false. This strategy denies that sentences of possible worlds are truth-apt (cf. Divers 2002, pp. 22-25). Simon Blackburn writes:

> In present terms, the issue must be one about how we explain our making of modal commitments. We certainly do not explain it by thinking that we are made sensitive to possibilities because of some quasi-sensory capacity which responds to the presence or absence of possible worlds. Firstly, since the only possible world that is actual is the actual world, others cannot *actually* influence us: we cannot receive information about them because there is nothing to actually influence any receptors. Ways things might have been cannot be seen or heard. Secondly, the position that we are simply describing different aspects of reality needs a supplementation which it finds hard to give. (Blackburn 1984, p. 214)

Blackburn asks how is it that modal statements are justified. His thesis is that no relationship between subject and possible worlds plays a role,

---

[14]I believe it is a pity for philosophers to avoid commitment due to insufficient literature.

having to do with lack of sensory perceptions of the subject. He justifies the thesis using antirealism, arguing that to think about possibilities and necessities in terms of related possible worlds is helpful because we want to know how to conduct ourselves. Hence, we must persist with using possible-world-talk, but he denies possible worlds, giving preference to a theory that maintains the benefits of possible-world-imagery without commitment to Lewisian worlds. A similar view is that modalities cannot coherently be represented, neither in possible worlds nor otherwise, which is popular. The reasons for this decision vary, but the most salient motivation is that philosophy of the modal is not served best by use of possible worlds because it is difficult to reduce modality. Gideon Rosen supports this type of theory.

(22) Gandalf leans on a staff.

(23) My grandpa leans on a staff.

The next strategy is to say that (22) will always be false (cf. Divers 2002, pp. 22-25). The ontological assumption of possible worlds is difficult to deal with, and it is easier to suppose that possible-world-talk is fiction. The difference between (22) and (23) is that Gandalf is a fictional character and grandpa is a real person. We speak of Gandalf despite the fact that he does not exist. We say that he leans on a staff, but we are not discussing a real person. Modal fictionalism is the view that we should analyse modal statements as the content of fiction. The statement "it is possible that P iff there is some world Δ, in which it is the case that P" is true if and only if P is true according to the hypothesis of possible worlds. Rosen argues that according to the hypothesis of a plurality of worlds, multiple worlds exist (cf. Rosen 1995, pp. 67-68). The claim that Gandalf exists does not depend on the existence of a world containing the wizard who is the leader of the Fellowship of the Ring. One objection against modal fictionalism is that fictions are incomplete (cf. Nolan 2016). Rose suggests that in fiction, much more is true than what is mentioned. Gandalf had, for example, many thoughts and memories, and John Tolkien did not write all of his thoughts and memories. A modal fictionalist employs the "according to" operator, which seems to be a modal notion and thus primitive, and consequently, an analysis of modality is not provided (cf. Nolan 2016). As Theodore Sider notes, the objection is that modal fictionalism does not reduce modality by "according to" expressing a modal notion when analysing modality (cf. Sider 2003, p. 14). I now consider contrasting theories and assess whether it is prudent to deepen abstentionism and antirealism.

3.1 Modal Realism

What do modal realists share in common? The answer is the propensity to proclaim the existence of possible worlds. Modal realists accept possible world sentences as truth-apt (cf. Divers 2002, p. 21). Lewis calls his thesis "modal realism", but his conception has little to do with the philosophical stance of "realism".[15] Although Lewis' theory suggests that there exist other worlds for real and other individuals inhabiting those worlds, I agree with differentiation from John Divers, and call Lewis' theory "genuine modal realism". Consequently, modal realism includes actualist modal realism and Lewis' theory. Modal realists argue that some modal sentences are true and that such sentences permit a valid inference to the existence of some possible world. The nature of possible worlds correlates with theoretical terms. Many conceptions of what a possible world is exist. Depending on which conception we use, we get various natures of possible worlds. (cf. ibid., p. 21). Many modal realists try to reduce modalities to non-modal terms, but achieving this goal is something else, and difficult to accomplish.

---

[15]Realism suggests that objects of knowledge are independent of the observer (cf. Miller 2014).

25

3.2   Actualist Modal Realism

A humorous quote from Kripke explains the notion of possible worlds:[16]

> A possible world isn't a distant country that we are coming
> across, or viewing through a telescope. Generally speaking, an-
> other possible world is too far away. Even if we travel faster
> than light, we won't get to it. A possible world is given by the
> descriptive conditions we associate with it. (Kripke 1988, p. 44)

The primary alternative to genuine modal realism is actualist modal realism. Modal actualists agree that there is only one actual world and possible
worlds are abstract. There is only this actual world in which we live, the
way things are, "but most people will agree there are other possible states
for the world to have" (Nolan 2005, p. 52). The universe might have a
different history, and possible worlds are these different histories that the
universe might have had. The actual world is absolutely actual in the
sense that it is the only possible world that correctly represents the universe. The idea is that possible worlds exist, but they are abstract entities
that represent ways this world could have been (cf. Lewis 1986, p. 136).
There are multiple kinds of actualist modal realism, where possible worlds
are identified with various kinds of abstract things. Lewis calls these possible worlds as abstract objects ersatz possible worlds.[17] Subsequent actualist authors give various explanations for what a possible world might
be. Alvin Plantinga argues that a possible world is "a possible state of
affairs" (cf. Plantinga 1976, p. 145). Robert Adams defines them as "maximal consistent sets of propositions" (cf. Divers 2002, p. 179). Richard
Jeffrey conceives them as "complete consistent novels" (cf. ibid., p. 179).

---

[16]I label the person who started relational semantics an actualist modal realist. Kripke
indicates what possible worlds are; he does not say much about them, but at least he
accepts their existence, and the clue lies in "descriptive conditions".

[17]*Ersatz* is German for *replacement*. Ersatzism is a synonym of actualist modal realism.

Peter Forrest treats possible worlds as "ways the world could be" (cf. Lewis 1986, p. 87). David Armstrong argues they are "collections of compossible facts" (cf. Armstrong 1989, p. 147). Cresswell characterises them as "sets of basic particular situations and subsets of space-time points" (cf. Cresswell 1979, p. 136). Both Armstrong and Cresswell argue that possible worlds are recombinations of basic ontological objects. Ersatz possible worlds are usually maximal consistent sets of abstract representations. For example, they are usually maximal consistent sets of sentences. If I say that it is possible that William Shakespeare did not write the works attributed to him, it is true because there is some ersatz world of this world (what we call the actual world) according to which another person wrote the works attributed to Shakespeare. A world in which animals talk would be identified with a set that includes the sentence "animals talk". Ersatz possible worlds are from a different nature.

3.2.1   Plantingan Modal Realism

Plantingan modal realism typically acts as a counterpoint to genuine modal realism. Possible worlds for Plantinga are maximal possible states-of-affairs, which are abstract, existing entities just like propositions. A state-of-affairs can either obtain or fail to obtain. For example, the state-of-affairs of humans having wings fails to obtain since we are not angels and the state-of-affairs humans belonging to the family of great apes obtains since it is our taxonomic family. A state-of-affairs is possible iff it is metaphysically possible for it to obtain (cf. Plantinga 1976, p. 144). One objection against Plantingan modal realism is the assumption that states-of-affairs exist necessarily and that maximal states-of-affairs exist. The problem is that Plantinga's possible worlds cannot be used in a reductive account of modality. Plantinga does not suggest how the representing operates.[18] He

---

[18]That is why Lewis thinks of him as favouring magical ersatzism. Lewis calls magical ersatzism the position that claims that the nature of possible worlds is to represent, but

states that possible worlds are states-of-affairs, and although a problem lies in explaining what states-of-affairs are, he accepts that some modalities remain unanalysed (cf. Plantinga 1976, p. 139). Plantinga argues that they are ways things might be, possibilities, propositions, or structures belonging to our world. This position has the advantage that states-of-affairs associate with roles in our thought; it is easier to believe that maximal possible states-of-affairs exist. It is true though that we still do not have a notion about what type of entities possible worlds are.

3.2.2 Combinatorialism

Quine suggests that a possible world is a mathematical representation. We represent spacetime points occupied by matter, but ontology requires only matter and the structure of classes of individuals (cf. Quine 1968, p. 12). Quine was first one to sketch combinatorialism: "A possible world, finally can be explained in somewhat the same way but with four dimensions, representing space-time. A possible world becomes, roughly, any class whose members are all the classes that are geometrically similar to some one class of number quadruples" (Ibid., p. 14). Lewis does not identify world with any mathematical representation (cf. Lewis 1986, pp. 86-92). Cresswell first held a combinatorialist account, a recombination of certain metaphysical simples. Combinatorialists take possible worlds to be recombinations of elements. Circularity is avoided by giving a combinatorial definition of a possible world. Cresswell (as Quine does) takes possible worlds to be sets of spacetime points, and each set represents possibilities. All spacetime points are occupied with abstract matter, and the combinatorial nature of set theory gives rise to possible worlds. This type of actualist modal realism has a reduction that is clearly non-modal. We have these coordinates with which any pattern is possible. If we identify worlds with sets

it is not explained how possible worlds represent (cf. Lewis 1986, p. 141).

of spacetime points, modality is eliminated. Combinatorialism is based on the Leibnizian conception. A proposition is possible if and only if it is *true in* some possible world. A counterargument is that modality reappears in the definition of "true in". Note that combinatorialism cannot dispose of possibility and necessity. The problem lies in circularity when accepting that modality reappears when saying "true in". Based on Ludwig Wittgenstein's *Tractatus Logico-philosophicus*, Brian Skyrms proposes:

> Possible worlds are collections of compossible facts. We think about possible facts and possible worlds in two quite different ways. For possible worlds whose objects and relations are subsets of this world our possibilities are essentially *combinatorial*. We rearrange some or all of our relationships between some or all of the objects to get our possibilities. (Skyrms 1981, p. 201)

Inspired by Skyrms, Armstrong offers the most developed theory of combinatorialism, in which possible worlds are sets (i.e., conjunctions) of fundamental states-of-affairs. States-of-affairs involve particulars and universals. He has a preference for a fictionalist form of combinatorialism (cf. Armstrong 1989, p. 49). The world Armstrong begins with contains simple individuals (i.e., particulars), simple because they do not have individuals as proper parts. The world also contains simple properties (i.e., universals), simple because they lack proper constituents (cf. ibid., p. 38). Particulars and universals are constituents of the states-of-affairs. We have various elements, all those we have in our actual world such as headphones, music, and dancing, so a possible world is a recombination of existing elements and relations. We rearrange a world containing headphones and dancing, but not music. This would be a possibility without music (where life would be a mistake). Such a combination does not exist, and life cannot be a mistake in a possible world without music because we are talking only about logical possibilities.

3.2.3   Nature Modal Realism

The problem in this type of actualist modal realism is underdeveloped. We know only that world-natures are a special structural property because they are complete properties of maximal individuals. So, a possible world is a possible way things could have been for the entire cosmos. A third type of ersatzism is nature modal realism, advocated by Robert Stalnaker. Nature modal realism sees possible worlds as world-natures, world-properties, or ways our world might have been. The actualised world is the only world-nature that is instantiated. A nature realist will talk about properties, instantiations (of properties by individuals), conjunctions (form properties), and completions (for higher-order properties) (cf. Divers 2002, p. 177), and this is how modal realists explain what possible worlds are.

3.2.4   Book Modal Realism

The book modal realism proposes that possible worlds are like stories; their elements are propositions of a language. A world-story is a maximal consistent set of propositions in a language that has one member for every pair of mutually contradictory propositions, and all of its members can be true together (cf. Adams 1974, p. 225). We have this conception of world-books, and this means that worlds associate with books that describe the worlds. Books do the theoretical work, avoiding commitment to the described worlds. The lexicon for some world-making language consists of existing elements that generate sentences. Name, predicate, sentence, and consistency are the basic theoretical terms of book modal realism (cf. Divers 2002, pp. 178-180). The following questions demonstrate at what points doubt arises. Is the lexicon infinite? Are there infinite predicates and connectives? Is infinity constrained to countability? These types of factors determine the power of the world-making language. The Lagadonian language comes into play, in which it is stipulated that every individual is a name of itself, creating infinite sentences. This is the solution that Carnap adopts when he introduces "state-descriptions", trying to make sense of Leibniz' biconditionals, but he does not use infinite sentences. A "state-description" in a Lagadonian language represents construction from predicates and the negation symbol, in which each member serves its own name. State-descriptions could be considered ersatz possible worlds (cf. Lewis 1986, p. 145). Lewis' objections are that there are inconsistent descriptions, so we must distinguish the consistent ones. We cannot have two indiscernible descriptions, and we do have indiscernible parts of worlds. What can be described is limited by what we can have words for, but none of these problems arise for his genuine modal realism (cf. ibid., p. 165).

3.3   Concreteness or abstractness?

"Abstract" is the counter-term to "concrete". Abstract and concrete divide entities into disparate kinds. Plants and fruits are concrete entities. Numbers and freedom are abstract entities. Concrete entities are existent things (in reality), indiscernible and defined.[19] Concrete entities are simply given. We can causally interact with concrete entities; I can smell a flower or eat chocolate. Concrete entities are physical. Abstract entities are apart from reality or theoretical concepts; they have no spatiotemporal location, are never indiscernible, and do not enter causal interaction. Something abstract is an abstraction from a concrete entity. Propositions, universals (e.g., properties or relations), and mathematical objects (e.g., sets or structures) are abstract entities. There is no sensory perception of them; we cannot see them, and we cannot find them anywhere. Abstract entities lack change. Possible worlds are ways that the world could be. So, are possible worlds concrete or abstract? Concreteness and abstractness are

---

[19]Leibniz' law of the identity of indiscernibles dictates that if for every property F, x exemplifies F iff y exemplifies F, then x and y are identical (cf. Zalta 2011, p. 6).

competing perspectives regarding what possible worlds are. If we imagine a world and the limits of all the situations going on, it is possible to consider concrete or abstract what the situations are taken to be (cf. Menzel 2016). The concretist intuition proceeds by thinking that all situations of the world are physical and that other worlds are from the same kind. For concretists, possible worlds are concrete physical, no different in kind from the actual world. Abstractionism leads to other intuitions; the situations are not physical, but exist as states or conditions. For abstractionists, a possible world is a total way things could be, "a consistent state to which no further detail could be added without rendering it inconsistent" (Ibid.) Lewis resists the concept of concreteness and abstractness (cf. Lewis 1986, pp. 81-86); he does not understand what is meant by "concrete" and "abstract," so he denies claiming that possible worlds are concrete. He agrees with the concept, but prefers to explain that other worlds are of a kind with this world of ours. Lewis resists the concept of concreteness and abstractness because other worlds would also have abstract entities and not only concrete individuals. The distinction between concrete and abstract is parallel to the distinction between individuals and sets. Lewis argues that worlds are individuals and not sets, so it is plausible to say that worlds are concrete.

3.4 Genuine Modal Realism

Mentioned above, Lewis holds that there is an infinite number of worlds, say spatiotemporal and causally isolated, and ours is just one. He describes possible worlds as:

> There are countless other worlds, other very inclusive things. Our world consists of us and all our surroundings, however, remote in time and space; just as it is one big thing having lesser

things as parts, so likewise do other worlds have lesser other-worldly things as parts. The worlds are something like remote planets; except that most of them are much bigger than mere planets, and they are not remote. Neither are they nearby. They are not at any spatial distance whatever from here. They are not far in the past or future, nor for that matter near; they are not at any temporal distance whatever from now. They are isolated: there are no spatiotemporal relations at all between things that belong to different worlds. Nor does anything that happens at one world cause anything to happen at another. Nor do they overlap; they have no parts in common, with the exception, perhaps, of immanent universals exercising their characteristic privilege of repeated occurrence. (Lewis 1986, p. 2)

This definition made Lewis famous, or perhaps infamous, but genuine modal realism is one of the greatest reduction programs. The advantage of Lewis' theory is that it reduces the modal to non-modal. The disadvantage is that it requires ontological commitment to a multiverse.[20]

3.4.1 Lewis' Analysis of Possible Worlds.

A world can be defined as:

$\forall \Delta$ (Δ is a world iff Δ is an individual $\wedge \forall \alpha$ ($\forall \omega$ (((α is a part of Δ $\wedge$ ω is a part of Δ) $\rightarrow$ (There is some spatiotemporal relation in which α stands to ω)) $\wedge$ ((α is part of Δ $\wedge$ there is some spatiotemporal relation R in which α stands to ω) $\rightarrow$ (ω is part of Δ)))))) (cf. Divers 2002, p. 86)

This definition lies at the core of Lewis' modal realism. A set of possible worlds exists, and a world is an individual comprised of the sum of parts

---

[20]The hypothetical set of an infinite number of possible worlds or parallel universes.

that can also be considered individuals. Individuals are parts of the same world if they share spacetime (i.e., they relate spatiotemporally). The following image expounds the concept of possible worlds. We are certain that this situation is only part of a series of increasingly more inclusive situations. This room is a whole – citywide in Germany, in Europe, the Earth, the solar system, the galaxy, etc. (cf. Menzel 2016) – until we see the pattern of a fractal and a plurality of worlds.

> On the face of it, anyway, it seems quite reasonable to believe that this series has a *limit*, that is, that there is a maximal inclusive situation encompassing all others: *things, as a whole* or, more succinctly, *the actual world*. (Ibid.)

Now comes the great reduction. According to genuine modal realism, ontological primitives are either sets or individuals. A world is the mereological sum of individuals; a world is the totality of things. Each individual is part of exactly one world, and relates spatiotemporally to other individuals in that world. Apart from this, Lewis makes other presumptions. I now examine Lewis' central doctrines regarding possible worlds.

Isolation

There is a boundary between worlds; every world is isolated because there are no spatiotemporal relations between one world and another. A consequence of Lewis' position is isolation. Worlds must be isolated so that in the passing of their own independent time, different events occur. A counterexample exists – worlds that overlap. Lewis is against overlap; he argues that worlds have no parts in common, and each thing is part of only one world (cf. Lewis 1986, p. 88). There are different ways of how a world could be.[21] The many-worlds interpretation does not appear on the higher

---

[21]Modal metaphysicians do not support a many-worlds view alone. Some physicists argue that such a view is required for correct interpretation of quantum mechanics, but

Lewisian scale. He argues that worlds do not overlap. Lewis rejects a single world that consists of less isolated world-like-parts, impossible worlds, and empty worlds. A world on the higher Lewisian scale is not like a container, but rather a mereological sum of spatiotemporally interrelated individuals, and thus no absolutely empty world exists. Lewis' opinion is that there is no world in which there is nothing, and this explains why there is something rather than nothing. Besides the idea of spatiotemporal relations, there is also no causation between worlds, which is another reason that worlds must be isolated. Causation within a world occurs like this: in world Δ, we have two events. The first causes the second, but if the first event had not been, the second would have never occurred (cf. Lewis 1986, pp. 69-81). Lewis' concept of causation is explained in terms of counterfactual dependence. Suppose Antonio orders a pizza and then a delivery employee knocks on the door. If Antonio had not ordered the pizza, the delivery employee would not have knocked. The employee knocking on the door depends causally on Antonio ordering the pizza (cf. ibid., p. 23).

Actuality

The concept of actuality is the next important tenet for Lewis' position of possible worlds. The actual world is the world of context. Lewis uses the word "actual" like "this-worldly." Actuality is an indexical term like "I," "you," "here," or "now." For example, "I" refers to whomever is speaking. If an individual belongs to some world of context, the individual is actual in that world, meaning that the actual world is the world of which we are parts. Our actual world is just one among a plurality of worlds, and no world has a privileged ontological status. Inhabitants of other worlds call

it is not exactly the same view. The many-worlds interpretation – due to (Hugh Everett III – has to do with timelines branching and defeating the laws of identity and non-contradiction, in which a cat can be both alive and dead. It is as if there were different scales. On the Lewisian scale of possible worlds, we have these isolated worlds, but each world at a lower scale can have different features like an Everett's many-branched tree.

their worlds actual. There is a plurality of worlds. Our world is actual and the others are unactualised. A world of our counterparts would be actual for them and is unactualised for us. When a speaker uses the word "actual," he/she refers to his/her world. "Actual" is analogous to "present" because they are indexical terms. Every world is actual in itself. We have the knowledge that we are actual; we are not the select few. No world is absolutely actual; it is relative which world is actual, and varies from world to world (cf. Lewis 1986, pp. 92-96). Reducing reality to sets and individuals constitutes Lewis' reductionism. Reality includes much more than what we see in this world; "only this-worldly things really exist is *restricted* speaking". The totality of white tigers that are spatiotemporally related to us does not exhaust the totality of white tigers in existence. This includes all tigers of all colours in the visible spectrum, and even talking and flying tigers exist *simpliciter*. What Lewis is saying is that the quantifiers are unrestricted. Just because the alcoholic beverages run out at a party does not mean that alcoholic beverages have run out in the world (cf. ibid., p. 3); there are certainly more alcoholic beverages in other places. Quantifiers range over actual and non-actual individuals. Just because dinosaurs went extinct does not mean they have gone extinct in other worlds. Lewis uses the word "actual" generally. If numbers are part of this world, they are actual because they are parts of this world. The same applies to properties, defined as subsets of the set of all individuals. Propositions are defined as the subsets of the set of all worlds. An event is the property of being a spatiotemporal region, and hence we can call properties, propositions (at least the true propositions), and events actual (cf. ibid., p. 95).

Plenitude

An important tenet is the principle of recombination, which states that patching together parts of different possible worlds yields another possible world. As long as individuals occupy different spatiotemporal positions, anything can coexist with anything else (cf. Lewis 1986, p. 87). Copied parts of a world can make up another world, and other worlds are comprised of copied parts of our world. We can therefore deduce indiscernible possible worlds from the principle of recombination.[22] There should not be gaps in logical space. We need to ensure that there are sufficient possibilities. Where a world might have been, there is a world (cf. ibid., p. 86). Lewis proposes that every possibility is a way for some world to be, and tries to be precise about the principle of plenitude with this proposal. He rejects the proposal of identifying possible worlds with possibilities, though it is advantageous. The proposal does not suggest that there is an infinite number of possible worlds. If possible worlds must cover every way that a world could possibly be, we say only that each of the unit sets has a member (a unit set is a maximal specific "way"). Lewis uses the principle of recombination to guarantee the plenitude of worlds, related to "the Humean denial of necessary connections between distinct existences" (Ibid., p. 86), which means the failure of anything coexisting with anything else. The Humean principle suggests that everything can exist with everything, but does not have to. We cannot say that every way we think that a world could possibly be is a way that some world is. Significantly, other possible worlds will exist and our opinion will neither affect nor change them.

---

[22]Haecceitism argues that worlds can differ in some non-qualitative way, without differing qualitatively. Anti-haecceitism is the counter position, suggesting that such indiscernible possible worlds are impossible (cf. Skow 2008, p. 99).

3.4.2 Counterpart Theory

Counterpart Theory is not part of Lewis' definition of possible worlds, though it is prominent in his theory of possible worlds. Lewis suggests that nothing is in anything, except a world. Nothing is in two worlds and nothing is a counterpart of anything else in its world (cf. Lewis 1968, p. 114). If two individuals are part of the same world, they are world-mates. Worldmates from another world make up a different world. We have counterparts in those other Lewisian worlds (who resemble us). The counterpart relation is neither transitive nor symmetrical. If x_0 in W_0 has a counterpart x_1 in W_1 that has a counterpart x_2 in W_2, x_2 is the counterpart of x_0 only and only if they also resemble closely, but x_0 and x_2 do not have to be counterparts. This shows that the counterpart relation is not transitive. If x_0 is similar to x_1 and x_1 is similar to x_2, x_0 can be dissimilar to x_2, or as Lewis writes: "Little differences add up to big differences" (Lewis 1986, p. 219). The antecedent is similar to the subsequent, but after many little changes, we get a different individual. That is why the counterpart relation has to be intransitive. But why should it not be symmetrical? x_a and x_b are twins in W_0, and x_b has counterpart x_c in W_2, but if the resemblance between x_c and x_b is far closer than between x_c and x_a, x_a is not a counterpart of x_c. x_b is related to x_a and x_c, but x_a and x_c are not related. The counterpart relation is asymmetrical, otherwise they would all be related (cf. ibid., p. 116). Similarities across possible worlds determine a counterpart relation. Lewis suggests a counterpart relation instead of transworld individuals. If identity is shared between individuals in different possible worlds, the individuals would be transworld individuals. Lewis is against transworld identity, in part because of complications with transworld causation and mereological sums. Lewis replaces transworld identity by counterpart relations. A world is the mereological sum of all individuals who are parts of the world. Individuals can be counterparts and exactly alike, maybe up to some time and then differ at some point. Two worlds can be exactly alike up to some time and diverge thereafter. The initial segments are duplicates. Two things are duplicates iff they have the same properties or their parts can be put into correspondence (cf. Lewis 1986, p. 61). Counterparts are similar to each other. A siren cannot be the counterpart of an imp since their surrounding worlds do not match, but the imp and siren can have duplicate molecules because duplication is about shared properties. Counterpart theory describes individuals as being very similar, individuals in different worlds that have the same origins, which are often decisive for how an individual will develop in later life. Two counterparts can be different in so many ways if their early years go differently, and two duplicates always share the same properties (cf. ibid., p. 89).

Counterpart Theory Applied

The genuine modal interpretation of possible worlds proceeds in distinct ways that depend on whether it is dealt with a case of *de dicto* or *de re* modality (cf. Divers 2002, p. 43). With his counterpart theory, Lewis solves the problem facing *de dicto* and *de re* modalities. Depending on whether dealing with *de dicto* or *de re* phrases, genuine modal realism proceeds as:

(24) There might be a goddess who is the embodiment of love.

(25) Aphrodite might have been queen of the gods.

Sentence (24) is read *de dicto*. In the *de dicto* interpretation, world ("Wx") is construed first, and the existence of a goddess who is the embodiment of love ("$Gy \wedge Ly$") at the world is construed as the world having the goddess in its parts ("Pyx").

$$\exists x \, \exists y \, (Wx \wedge Pyx \wedge Gy \wedge Ly)$$

Sentence (25) faces a *de re* interpretation. The existence of a world is construed again as the existence *simpliciter*. However, for the world to represent that Aphrodite is queen of gods, a counterpart of Aphrodite is needed ("Cya") that represents Aphrodite being queen of the gods ("Qy").

$$\exists x\,\exists y\,(Wx \wedge Pyx \wedge Cya \wedge Qy)$$

Modal facts are existential. There is at least a possible world for every possibility. If we say that the goddess Aphrodite might exist, the existence of Aphrodite is the truth-maker for the modal claim. It is possible that P iff there is some world Δ such that in Δ, P. This sentence addresses the normal case in which P is restricted to individuals who coexist in the same spacetime.

3.4.3 Arguments in Favour of Genuine Modal Realism

The world could be different than it is; it could end tomorrow or it could be a better place. We are faced with choices in everyday life, and we try to take the best options and opportunities. Decisions are made every moment. Possible worlds correspond to our daily opinions about alternatives and strategies about the fact that there are other ways of how things could be. It is obviously a risky hypothesis, though great achievements involve great risks. A plurality of worlds exists because the concept of possible world emerged to define possibility, and there are endless possibilities. When we talk about possibilities, we are imagining a possible world in which such alternatives occur. Through language we describe how other possible worlds are. Other possible worlds exist because we think about them, and this is a reason to believe in a plurality of worlds. Possible worlds have become a widely used philosophical term. We talk as if possible worlds would exist, and natural language that expresses modal statements is a sign that other worlds exist. Modal logic is intentional. We can talk about what could have been using the concept of possible worlds. Genuine modal realism has the great advantage that modal discourse is extensional. There are references to the terms in other worlds. If I say that I could have had brown eyes, I am talking about a counterpart of me that has brown eyes. The extension embraces all of my brown-eyed counterparts. The strongest argument that can be advanced to support genuine modal realism is the achievement of modal reductionism. Modal terms can be defined in non-modal terms. If we talk about possibilities, we can secure our ability to express modalities if we begin with primitives that are not modal. A theory with the least possible primitives is better, and we can reduce everything to individuals and set-theoretic constructions of them. Due to modal reductionism, we can accept our modal opinions. If y would have happened, z would have happened. We have a "powerful tendency to think in modal terms" (Plantinga 1987, p. 202), and modal reductionism allows us to believe that things might have been different. Most people believe that things might have been different. Genuine modal realism is the only theory that achieves modal reductionism. Lewis achieves the reduction of modality, because he says that other worlds exist. Hence, he is saying that modality expresses what happens in other worlds, and other worlds are of the same kind as our world, which is not a modal concept. What really happens is not modal anymore. He defines modality with something that is like our world. Another theory that offered the same advantages, without having to assume a plurality of worlds, would be the winner. The strongest arguments *pro tempore* are provided by genuine modal realism. We get a concept at the underlying ground of our philosophical theories that allows us to define all other concepts (in lieu of having many qualitative concepts at the underlying ground). The reduction program is worth a never-ending quantity of worlds. Lewis has another reason, which is that the hypothesis is serviceable. He calls possible worlds a paradise for philosophers, just as David Hilbert calls sets a paradise for mathematicians. The hypothesis that possible worlds are fruitful[23] is a good reason to believe they exist.

---

[23]Many interpretations and formalisms using possible worlds exist so ordinary language can be analysed logically since the construction of a formal language is required. This is

But, why not just accept that possible worlds are abstract objects? It is an option to think that possible worlds, sets, and numbers are just conceptual tools, this position is called instrumentalism. Instrumentalism is opposed to scientific realism, the latter states that reality exists independent of human thought and that science can tell us what reality looks like. In accordance with scientific realism, Lewis argues that his theory offers a far-reaching approach.

3.5 Critique of Genuine Modal Realism

I now turn to the critique. Aside from the difficult digestion of a plurality of worlds, one objection is that if modal facts are existential, too many modal truths are being accepted. The answer to this objection is that possibilities are not always possible worlds; possible worlds are some of the possibilities (cf. Lewis 1986, p. 230). The critique has to do with Lewis misunderstanding his own position. Critics warn of problems ahead, suggesting caution. They suggest that Lewis misrepresents the possible as impossible in cases concerning (a) quantification over non-actuals, (b) disconnected spacetimes and temporally disconnected dual existences, (c) island universes, (d) alien spatiotemporal relations, and (e) the principle of recombination. Beyond these questions concerning the world's nature, there are complaints about

---

the major application of logic. In the case of modal logic, modal concepts are elucidated. Modal logic has become increasingly important in all fields of philosophy, and there are nearly no limits. Modal logic is very important to the philosophy of logic, metaphysics, semantics, ethics, probability theory, philosophy of language, philosophy of mind, philosophy of science, and many other contexts. However, modal logic is not only important in philosophy, but also mathematics, linguistics, and computer and information sciences (cf. Cocchiarella and Freund 2008, p. 5). Deontic, temporal, and epistemic logics have been formalised in modal logic. Logicians, philosophers, and computer scientists benefit most from modal logic. Logicians want to capture the notions of possibility, logical necessity, and proof. Philosophers, quantum physicists, and artificial intelligence researchers have interests in questions regarding planning and time. Dynamic logic is an application generated by computer scientists who apply modal logic to processes in machines (cf. Girle 2009, p. 137).

(f) unanalysed modalities, (g) counterpart relations, and (h) the epistemology of worlds.

(a) Some say that Lewis offers a Meinongian ontology (e.g., William Lycan refers to genuine modal realism as "Lewis' branch of Meinongianism") (Lycan 1979, p. 287). A meinongian ontology accepts that there are objects that do not exist. Critics argue over Lewis' Meinongian commitment to non-existent objects. To be able to say that an object does not exist, we must presuppose its existence. Their arguments demonstrate that Lewis suggests that there is an object x that does not exist in the actual world. Therefore, x does not exist. Genuine modal realism rejects that there is an object in the actual world that does not exist. All objects in the actual world exist, and all objects in other possible worlds also exist. Existential quantification over an unrestricted, maximal domain of individuals has no problem (cf. Divers 2002, pp. 60-62). Lewis does not support quantification ranging over entities that do not exist, including possibilia and impossibilia. He supports only quantification ranging over non-actual possibilia. Genuine modal realism has still to admit *sui generis* entities and the theory requires also for it to be possible that sets exist. Lewis' strategy explains that existence in a world is a generic relation, meaning an entity is in a world by being part of it. He does not suggest that sets are parts of worlds; instead, he says that sets of actual things are actual (cf. Lewis 1986, p. 94).

(b) The next problem that is counterintuitive is the position of disconnected times (cf. Rosenberg 1989, p. 412). Immanuel Kant considered this position absurd (cf. Kant 2003, A127). Genuine modal realism still entails commitment to the existence of disconnected times as a possibility. Kantian position applies in our actual world. In this sense, Lewis and Kant agree that a world with two disconnected spacetimes is impossible. Another critic (see King 1995) suggests that precisely because Lewis and Kant agree, genuine modal realism is bound to misrepresent the possible as impossible. The concept of temporally disconnected dual existences advocates that a subject experiences two alternate lives in disconnected times, and that genuine modal realism should change from a temporal to causal account of worlds. However, the concept of world is prior to that of the causal relation in definitions given by Lewis. Causation is analysed in terms of counterfactuals that are analysed in terms of truth values across spheres of proximate worlds, and proximity is analysed in terms of similarity. Truth conditions of counterfactuals refer to possible worlds. (cf. Divers 2002, pp. 90-92).

(c) Intuitively, it is possible that individuals exist who interrelate spatiotemporally. According to Lewis, this is impossible because parts of a world relate spatiotemporally. Some metaphysicians embrace island universes. For example, Phillip Bricker argues that physical reality might have isolated parts. Bricker analyses modal operators as plural quantifiers instead of individual quantifiers, and the result is universal actualization and the possibility of nothing (cf. Bricker 2001, p. 27). Lewis cannot deny the possibility of island universes, meaning worlds that are spatiotemporally and causally isolated but co-actual, but he undermines those intuitions, claiming that this point does not have consequences regarding what is possible (cf. Lewis 1986, p. 71).

(d) A world with Newtonian spacetime is possible.[24] How would spatiotemporal relations behave in such a world? The question is how to handle non-actual spatiotemporal relations. When we use the term *spatiotemporal*, we cover only worlds in which our spatiotemporal re-

---

[24]There is not only relative time and space, but also absolute time and space (Rynasiewicz 2014).

lations are instantiated. Lewis suggests that the relations are natural (i.e., not disjunctive), pervasive (i.e., direct relatedness within systems is transitive), discriminating (i.e., interrelated individuals who are discernible), and external (i.e., relations supervene only on the intrinsic natures of the relata) (cf. Lewis 1986, pp. 75-76). Lewis plays with the idea of replacing relativistic spatiotemporal relations to define the worlds together. Each world interrelates by relations that are analogous to spatiotemporal relations.

(e) According to the principle of recombination, a possible world can be comprised of parts of other possible worlds. It appears that a principle of recombination is indispensable to genuine modal realism because enough worlds are needed to guarantee extensional veracity, and thus all of the plenitude of possibilities can be captured. The unrestricted principle entails problems. Forrest and Armstrong formulate a paradox that endangers the existence of a set of all individuals – a world Δ that contains duplicates of all objects. The paradox arises by *reductio ad absurdum*. A world copies a class of possible individuals, and the bigger the classes, the bigger the worlds can be (cf. ibid., p. 102). Assume a world with n electrons. It is possible that the members of each subset of the n electrons have *F-ness*. A set of worlds must then contain possible worlds with electrons corresponding to each of the subsets. *F-ness* is added to the members of the subsets of electrons and we get 2^n of these worlds (cf. Armstrong 1989, p. 26). Lewis proposes a restricted version of the principle of recombination. A world can be filled with duplicates of individuals, but there is a principle called "size and shape permitting" that states that there is a limited number of individuals who cannot exceed the infinite cardinal number of points in a spacetime continuum (cf. Lewis 1986, p. 89). The restricted version of the principle of recombination assumes that the duplication of individuals is kept within limits by the maximum size of existing spacetime. Daniel Nolan offers a cardinality (i.e., the number of members of a set) argument that threatens a set of all possible individuals (cf. Nolan 1996, p. 246). Nolan argues that the paradox raised by Forrest and Armstrong is invalid and that the unrestricted principle of recombination is more intuitive than the restricted one (cf. ibid., p. 255). The consequence is that for each number of elements of set x, it is possible that there are at least x urelements[25] (cf. Uzquiano 2015, p. 2). Genuine modal realism must persist with an unrestricted principle of recombination and the denial of the existence of a set of all individuals, and operate with a maximal sum of all individuals as a proper class being construed as a set-like that has all the members available but is not itself a member of any class (cf. Divers 2002, pp. 101-103).

(f) Some critics argue that Lewis does not provide non-modal analyses of modal and intentional concepts. Theoretical terms (i.e., world, individual, set, sum, part of, member of, and spatiotemporally related to) of modal realism are implicitly modal, and if this is true, genuine modal realism is only a fairy tale. The truth is that none of the theoretical terms is modal. Genuine modal realism generates a plurality of worlds. The question is whether this set is consistent (i.e., to disqualify the existence of impossible worlds). Scott Shalkowski argues that genuine modal realism is either arbitrary and stipulative, or circular. Shalkowski says that even if there were Lewisian worlds, they would not provide grounds for modality (cf. Shalkowski 2014, p. 2). The answer depends on the intuitions that we have. Are modal facts prior to facts about non-actual worlds? Shalkowski says yes because worlds have modal features or because of modal restrictions on the nature

---

[25]Objects of the universe of all sets that are not sets.

of the worlds. Divers argues that worlds have such modal features; it has nothing to do with priority, only modality (cf. Divers 2002, p. 113). Shalkowski prefers actualist modal realism because modality is neither reducible nor eliminable (cf. Shalkowski 2014, p. 11).

(g) There are many questions in Lewis' counterpart theory (e.g., your counterpart resembles you more closely than other individuals). Some say that facts about counterparts of an individual are irrelevant to the modal truth about the individual (cf. Divers 2002, p. 125). If I say that I might have studied physics, am I talking about me or someone else? Lewis says that I am talking about me, and that I would satisfy the claim if I have a counterpart that studies physics. Where is my counterpart, and how can I access my counterpart? Lewis says that we cannot access other worlds.

(h) The last critique of genuine modal realism that I discuss is epistemological. How do we know that there are other possible worlds? Lewis argues that the hypothesis has utility, and that is why we should believe it is true. Lewis compares his case with mathematics. Do we have mathematical knowledge? If we say yes, how is it justified? The answer relies on its serviceability. Lewis claims that we have modal knowledge that does not require causal acquaintances with the objects of knowledge. He accepts that he cannot create truth through declaration; "whatever the truth may be, it isn't up to us" (cf. Lewis 1986, p. 114).

3.6   Neo-Meinongianism

According to Alexius Meinong, metaphysics is the science whose function deals with objects, and has to do with everything that exists. The totality of what exists, including what has existed and will exist, is smaller than the totality of objects of knowledge, and ideal objects do not exist and cannot be real, but they do subsist. Some examples are similarity, difference, ideas, assumptions, judgments, numbers, etc. (cf. Meinong 1960, p. 79). His theory of objects is different from the other sciences and metaphysics because it is the theory of nonexistent objects. Meinong was interested in intentional states not directed at anything existent. Sometimes people imagine, admire, dream, desire, or fear nonexistent things. Meinong solves the problem by saying that there is an object for every mental state. Meinong propounds the view that mental phenomena are connected with an intentional directedness toward an object. There are other reasons for believing that there are nonexistent objects (cf. Reicher 2015):

⋆ The problem with negative singular existence statements. To deny the existence of an individual, we must assume the existence of the individual. Consider:

(26) The minotaur does not exist.

The concept of nonexistent objects allows us to say (26) without having to say that they exist; we just say that minotaurs are the kind of objects that do not exist. This covers the next point.

⋆ The problem of fictional discourse:

(27) An alicorn is a winged unicorn.

All fictional characters and settings do not exist in real life. We are talking about something that does not exist now. This leads to:

⋆ The problem of discourse about the past and future:

(28) Heraclitus was a philosopher.

(29) In one hour, I will still be here.

If we talk about our human ancestors and we find fossils of hominins, in what way does the past exist? If Friedrich Nietzsche talks about the Übermensch,[26] in what form does the future exist? It seems that all we have is the present (everything in the past haunts a future that is made from steadily and progressively catching up with the present), but it is also clear that we can talk about past and future events, which appears paradoxical. We could say that in a sense, past and future exist, and in another that they do not. If we say that australopithecines[27] exist but they are not present anymore, what does it mean to exist? The answer to this is to say that they existed (in the simple past). Events in the past exist in simple past. The problem is that "to exist" means to have actual being or a life. This obviously means that australopithecines had life, but they do not have life anymore. If they do not exist anymore, they are nonexistent beings. Likewise, what can we do with inconsistent statements?

* The problem of alleged analytic truths:

(30) The round triangle is round and angular.

The last point is morally relevant.

* Nonexistent people in practical philosophy:

(31) Are people who never existed and will never exist morally relevant?

I have the intuition that someone who never existed and will never exist is still morally relevant. They represent existent people. The Meinongian approach is to say that they are nonexistent beings.

---

[26]Translates as *overhuman* and represents an ideal human in the future.
[27]An extinct genus of bipedal hominins that lived in Africa between two and four million years ago.

These examples belong to the world of the abstract. Meinongianism assumes nonexistent objects. A proponent of meinongianism pleads for the subsistence of objects that do not exist, and hence nonexistent objects do not exist, but they do subsist. By referring and quantifying these nonexistent objects, we say that there is something that is identical to them, so in a way, they have being. Meinong supports quantification ranging over entities that exist and do not exist (cf. Divers 2002, p. 59). He argues that independent of human thought, a realm of possibility exists because he took it to be obvious that there are nonexistent possibles and impossibles (cf. Lycan 1979, p. 275). Bertrand Russell at one time held a similar view to Meinong's. Every term for the Russell of *Principles of Mathematics* had being but not existence, only subsistence. After the *Principles of Mathematics* Russell gave up his view. Russell misinterpreted Meinong because Meinong does not claim that nonexistent objects have existence. Meinong also uses the term *bestehen* (to subsist) for nonexistent objects. In "On Denoting", Russell criticises that Meinong infringes on the law of non-contradiction (cf. Russell 1905, p. 483). Does spacetime contain a flying horse of flesh and blood, or is Pegasus only a mental Pegasus-idea? "On what there is", Quine criticises philosophers who limit the word *existence* to actuality. Only because it would be nonsense to say that Pegasus is not, such philosophers expand their ontology, but this overpopulated universe offends Quine's aesthetic sense. He calls such a universe overpopulated and unlovely (cf. Quine 1948, pp. 22-24). Quine argues that physical objects and mathematical objects are myths, but we should believe in them because they offer advantages when simplifying reports of our experiences (cf. ibid., p. 34). Terence Parsons defends neo-Meinongianism, admitting non-real objects in our actual world (cf. Parsons 1982, p. 365). He argues that we should believe in nonexistent objects for the same reason Quine believes in physical objects and mathematical objects – they simplify reports of our experiences in the same way (cf. ibid., p. 370). Another argument against nonexistent objects is that we cannot interact causally with them, and therefore we cannot know anything about them. Genuine modal realism and actualist modal realism suggest possible worlds exist. A reply to this objection given by Priest is that we cannot interact with possible worlds. Both genuine modal realists and actualist modal realists have no advantage over neo-Meinongianism (cf. Priest 2005, pp. 30-31). We know facts about nonexistent objects. For example, Sirens are beautiful, imps are uncontrollable, and both mythical creatures are dangerous. Priest claims that it is very simple; nonexistent objects do not exist. He also claims that possible worlds semantics is committed to neo-Meinongianism because it quantifies the objects in all domains, not the actual domain alone (cf. ibid., p. 14).

3.6.1 Meinongian Modal Realism

Takashi Yagisawa espouses Lewisian impossible worlds. I call such a position meinongian modal realism since impossible worlds are the kinds of things that do not exist. He believes that there could be impossible objects inhabiting impossible worlds. This is extended modal realism, a kind of Meinongian modal realism in which Lewis' theory is similar, only impossible worlds also exist. Impossible, concrete worlds sound strange. Something impossible cannot happen, so how could (why should) such a logical impossibility be instantiated? Yagisawa writes a humorous analogy:

> If Lewis' modal realism is healthy, the extended modal realism may be said to be *robust*. In comparison, we might say that actualist extensionalism is anemic, and non-extensionalists are, as it were, on a poisonous diet. (Yagisawa 1988, p. 183)

Yagisawa means by actualist extensionalism Kripke's semantic theory, it looks like an extensional semantic theory for an intentional modal logic, though it does not make modal logic extensional. Yagisawa's views rest on the assumption that concrete possible worlds offer an extensional theory of properties. He goes all the way with the primary theoretical premise behind him, that impossible worlds exist, resulting in ways that things could not have been. He argues that impossibilia cannot exist under any conditions, but they can exist under impossible conditions. Thereby he arrives at sets of worlds that are extensional, solving the granularity problem,[28] that is, how to deal with impossible propositions. Lewis deals with impossibilia using empty sets. Yagisawa calls ersatz impossible worlds "too moderate", and as if this were insufficient for the opponents to desire a boycott, there is logic behind it. For example, Greg Restall uses Priest's paraconsistent logic[29] to propose impossible worlds as sets of possible worlds. His reason is that many beliefs are inconsistent and do not belong to empty sets, but to different, non-empty sets. An example is a case of doublethink, in which Wolfgang believes that his life is run by fate and he must exercise freewill. A world could be consistent with fate and another with freewill, and then we could superimpose both worlds to get an impossible world. Wolfgang's belief is inconsistent, but he has a belief that is consistent in another world. Restall proposes that impossible worlds are more than one possible world taken together (cf. Restall 1997, p. 593). Restall does not believe that there are impossible worlds; he proposes paraconsistent logic to discriminate inconsistent beliefs. For monists who do not sympathise with logical pluralism[30] as Restall does, David Vander Laan offers another option – impossible worlds are maximal inconsistent classes of propositions. Vander Laan argues a theory of impossible worlds, but from an actualist perspective. He presents a Plantingan theory of impossible worlds. Vander

---

[28]The inability of possible world theories to make fine-grained distinctions for accounts of propositional attitudes (cf. Barwise 1997, p. 490). The granularity problem arises in theories of propositions, in which propositions are determined by truth conditions because it seems that individuals cannot believe in impossibilia.

[29]A logical system in which the principle of explosion (from contradiction, anything follows) does not apply.

[30]The thesis that there exists more than one correct logic.

Laan suspects that believing in possible worlds is also believing in impossible ones. Some states-of-affairs obtain like (32), others like (33) do not obtain but are possible, and others like (34) do not possibly obtain.

(32) You cannot say "M" without your lips touching.

(33) We have peace on Earth.

(34) To tell whether "this sentence is a lie" is true or false.

Impossible worlds are maximal impossible states-of-affairs. Vander Laan suggests that the arguments that have been offered for the existence of possible worlds also work similarly for the existence of impossible worlds. The first argument is that we can think of ways things could not have been, a subclass of states-of-affairs that cannot possibly obtain. We also have the argument from utility. Impossible worlds offer benefits of unity to the theory, and they help with analyses, during which possible worlds analyses are unsuccessful (cf. Laan 1997, pp. 597-600). Maybe concrete, impossible worlds are as Stalnaker comments: "Too much to swallow" (Stalnaker 1996, p. 193). Restall makes a point; it is a set of ways the world cannot be. Sometimes we take different objects to be the same, and sometimes we take the world inconsistently. What do we do when inconsistencies arise? The most plausible option for the common sense of classical logicians is Vander Laan's moderate modal realism. There is an ersatz impossible world for any way the world could not be since food that makes extended modal realism robust is too much to swallow.

3.7   Hybrid Modal Realism

Taking a middle-ground position, Francesco Berto claims that Lewisian worlds are the "basic stuff", and propositions are taken as sets of possible worlds. Impossible situations can be represented by world-books, sets of

Lewisian worlds. He is against the parity thesis, which suggests that there is no ontological difference between possible and impossible worlds. Priest explains the parity thesis:

> Any primary theory concerning the nature of possible worlds applies equally to impossible worlds: they are existent nonactual entities, they are nonexistent objects, they are constructions out of properties and other universals, and they are just certain sets of sentences. (Priest 1997, p. 580)

Impossible worlds are from the same kind as our preferred definition of possible worlds. An example is Yagisawa's extended modal realism (i.e., possible worlds are real and impossible worlds are real). Lewis is against the parity thesis because possible worlds are real, but impossible worlds do not exist. A proposition is a subset of the set of all worlds (cf. Lewis 1986, p. 53). World-books are maximal consistent sets of propositions, and Berto argues that they are sets of sets of Lewisian worlds; there should be no problem with inconsistent world-books representing impossibilities. He shows that a hybrid account offers genuine modal realism compelling arguments, and solves the granularity problem because impossible worlds help with impossible propositions. For example, one can have a world in which bachelors are married (cf. Berto 2010, p. 478). I return to what is possible and impossible. There are many distinct opinions, but we can assume that not everything is possible. We still have the availability of describing ways in which the world could not be. Why should there not be ways a world might not have been? That is why I cannot understand abstentionist motivations. We use modal statements commonly, and the Plantingan modal realism and nature modal realism must fight with un-analysed modalities and explain *obscurum per obscurius*. Berto proposes book modal realism since words can be taken as sets of concrete tokens. Berto does not discuss combinatorialism, which is weaker than the genuine rival. Genuine modal realism explains modality better due to a reduction of modality to talk of real worlds and regained extensionality while translating modal statements into talk about possible worlds. However, we have access only to set-theoretic constructions from words. Berto retains advantages of both worlds – ersatz and genuine. He promises that we are able to reduce propositions to extensional entities to avoid circularity, and discriminate impossible and possible propositions (cf. Berto 2010, p. 481). The solution begins with genuine modal realism (i.e., modal sentences are truth-apt because the quantification is over other worlds that exist), and then exploiting abstract set-theoretic constructions from genuine worlds as possible and impossible propositions. Hybrid modal realism is appealing to reductionists who endorse genuine modal realism. The advantage is distinguishing possible and impossible worlds, rejecting the parity thesis (i.e., possible worlds are real and impossible worlds are abstract). Hybrid modal realism demonstrates that possible worlds are concrete and impossible worlds are abstract. There is nothing against possible worlds being abstract too, and therefore possible worlds can be both concrete and abstract.

4

Evaluation

We have seen that there are different theories defining possible worlds. Both concretism and abstractionism provide clear definitions of possible worlds. Concretism achieves a reductive theory of modality, and abstractionism is a more intuitive account of what possible worlds are. I think that the concept of possible worlds promises successful explanations that illuminate the concept of modality. I defend genuine modal realism. But I think that for all concrete entities we can construct abstract entities. The world of the abstract is intriguing as well as other concrete possible worlds. I agree with Lewis that genuine modal realism is more economical, because the advantages are greater than those of actualist modal realism and the disadvantages are not greater that those afforded by actualist modal realism.

Berto holds a similar position as Lewis' genuine modal realism; "I could construct excellent ersatz worlds in ever so many ways, drawing on the genuine worlds for raw material; but he who believes in one concrete world only has no use for any of these constructions" (Lewis 1986, p. 186). Lewis does not need ersatz worlds, but he accepts that we can construct them. Lewis also expresses this from a combinatorial perspective: "However we should accept a correspondence: for every Quinean ersatz world, there is a genuine world with the represented pattern of occupancy and vacancy. This is just an appeal to recombination." (Lewis 1986, p. 90) Lewis also argues that inconsistent sets are ersatz impossible worlds: "An inconsistent set might be an ersatz impossible world, but it is not an ersatz possible world. Further, an ersatz world must be maximal consistent" (Ibid., p. 151). We refer to possible ways the world might be and impossible ways the world cannot be. The questions are: What is a possible world? Where are they? How do they work? Who creates and who perceives these possible worlds? Are they dreams inside of other dreams? Are they imagination? We could say yes to that practically and simplistically, or we could ask, "What is the difference between the concept of possible worlds and daydreaming?" Modal logic is the difference. Computer science works due to modal logic. We could say that the concept of possible worlds is still a more structured way of daydreaming, applied to a system; it is as easy as having an idea and applying it to a system. What is the difference? The system? Yes, the system makes the difference. When I read a book, I travel. I can see the trees, and I can see the forest. I am not really there. I am reading a system, again, letters on paper. The mind has the power to travel, and once we travel, we gain knowledge. With the visualization of different perspectives, we are gaining knowledge. I can visualise different ways of getting home. I can say, "If I take this route, it will last longer. Maybe there is more traffic, but if I take this other route, it is easier and I just have to make a turn here and so on." So I image both possibilities. I visualise my future and then act. I consider possibilities and which is best. Possible does not mean real. It is a parallel visualization about our actual world manifested in the mind, which is practical because we think about all these possibilities and then make something about it in our actual world. It is obvious to actualist modal realists that there are infinite possible worlds. It is obvious that there are many possibilities and parallel options available. We are constantly choosing and taking a path, and all the other paths are taken in an abstract way. If I play chess, I could imagine different possibilities and therefore act. All parallel paths are disposed of, and I just choose. In this way, I make the possibility real, but at the beginning, it was not real; just the concept of possibility is real. It is a practical way for reason to work. If we cannot perceive other possible worlds, it is difficult to understand them. This is one perspective, and it is like saying that possible worlds are not real; they are useful, but only in our minds. Is it all in the mind? Actualist modal realism provides an intuitive account of possible worlds at the expense of a reduction and extensional modal discourse. We could still say that Lewis criticises something that he belongs to – abstraction – because it is a visualization of him. Nevertheless, it is unfair to say that Lewis misunderstands his own position. I agree with Lewis; I do not argue that possible worlds exist only when we imagine them. Lewis' theory is not about proving that possible worlds exist, and nor does Lewis give conclusive arguments in favour of genuine modal realism. The central point is to accept that there are other ways of how our world could have been, and each befits a world that is that way. If we accept this last point, genuine modal realism allows the best explanation of modality. By thought experiments, and based on known things, we are persuaded to believe that other things are possible. Possible world is a concept that means an object of thought. They are products of mental activity. The different kinds of actualist modal realism are ways of reasoning, expressing, and imagining ways that the world could have been. In the same way, Berto offers a sketch of a theory regarding how actualist modal realism allows us to make discriminations about impossible worlds, that what cannot happen. I argue that the mind abstracts the concept of possible worlds from other concepts it already has such as possibility, spatiotemporal, sets, etc. For me, a plurality of really existing worlds is not too much to consider. Genuine modal realism is certainly the strongest theory and the best way to justify modal claims. I understand when most philosophers have akratic preferences (i.e., influenced by lack of empiricism). I defend genuine modal realism. Our world is not the only world that is actual. However, I consider this fact from this actual world. I exclude neither Lewisian nor ersatz worlds (and possible as impossible). My position can be expressed using two syllogisms:

1st: Our minds exist like this world exists.

Possible worlds exist in our minds
_____

Possible worlds exist like this world exists.

I defend the concept of possible worlds, at least from a Meinongian perspective. Possible worlds cannot escape subsistence, and they cannot escape existence either. The next question is whether they are concrete or abstract.

2nd: Sets of possibilia are concrete and abstract objects.

Possible worlds are sets of possibilia.
_____

Possible worlds are concrete and abstract objects.

Concrete or abstract, it is difficult to access other possible worlds. We have access only through ordinary language. Our world is concrete; it is not apart from reality. Hence, it is plausible that possible worlds are concrete. If I had to decide whether possible worlds are concrete or abstract, I would choose a concretist position, but I also believe that possible world is a theoretical concept, and we can construe ersatz possible worlds. What are possible worlds? *Possible worlds* are two words, meaning a totality of situations that happen or might happen. If they happen, we talk about Lewisian possible worlds. If we talk about possibilities that might happen, we can construe ersatz possible worlds. Possible worlds are concepts that refer to entities that could be a logical, metaphysical, or physical reality. Possible worlds are infinite and have individuals as parts. The counter term of possible worlds is impossible worlds, which do not exist, but we can certainly still talk about what does not exist, or even cannot exist. As far as we know, only our physical world exists, from which we are able to abstract other possible worlds. This does not take away the fact that Lewisian worlds could exist. We can compare possible worlds with thoughts. A person experiences only his or her own thoughts, without falling into solipsism. We do not know what it is to be someone else, and this does not consider the fact that other people exist with their own thoughts. I can only experience the actuality of my life, and thus possible worlds are actual abstractly, like someone being able to experience only his/her own life. And not because we are not able to experience lives of other people, it means that solipsism is reasonable. We perceive other people and cannot perceive other worlds. Can we perceive quarks of atoms? Is it worth believing in entities that our senses cannot perceive for the sake of the theory? It is understandable to be sceptical since these theories of possible worlds involve the existence of something that we cannot perceive and maybe even never verify.

Part III

Conclusion

5

Summary

Facts about how the world could, must or could not have been are facts about modality. I introduced modal logic. Next, I provided an insight into the different theories of possible worlds.

We could resume Lewis' theses in nearly the same way:

(i) Non-actual possible worlds exist just as real as our world.

(ii) Possible worlds are of the same kind as our actual world.

(iii) Quantifiers range over not only all the actual individuals, but also the non-actual individuals.

(iv) Every world is spatiotemporally and causally isolated from other worlds.

Lewis reduces modality to possible worlds by arguing that they exist, and each world is a mereological sum of its parts. Possible worlds are like our world. *De dicto* modalities are quantifiers over possible worlds, and possible worlds are not defined by modal concepts. Modality can be reduced (it is preferable), and so I agree with Lewis. My favourite view is a hybrid account, rescuing the advantages of both genuine modal realism and actualist modal realism.

6

Final Thoughts

Everything is debatable,[31] and it often depends on the viewpoint. I take a modal metaphysical viewpoint. The actualist versions of modal realism reduce possible worlds to abstract concepts. It is obvious that many possibilities exist. He also argues that there are more possibilities than abstract states-of-affairs, hypothetical spacetime points, fanciful world-natures, and fictional sentences. Some ersatzist views do not reduce to non-modal terms. Actualist modal realism deals with primitive modalities because all attempts at reduction have failed. We cannot take credit for actualist modal realism because the truth is that so far, it is all that we have. It is a serious problem speculating on a dogmatic theory, leaving us in the unknown. There will never be physical evidence that Lewisian worlds exist because they are causally isolated. I am skeptical. People believed that the sun, moon, stars, and naked-eye planets circled the earth. Theories from Nicolaus Copernicus and Johannes Kepler were metaphysical, because, at that time, they had few clues that did not count as empirical evidence; they lacked technology that demonstrated that their theories were correct. Little by little, we realized that not everything circles around us. But nevertheless, this is a disanalogy, because heliocentricism fulfilled the ver-

---

[31]Debatable that *everything* is debatable.

ifiability criterion, which Lewisian worlds do not fulfill. Because of that, heliocentricism and Lewisian worlds are not metaphysics in the same sense.

Theories of possible worlds rely on the first assumption that the course of history might have been different. I like to imagine that "the being" includes other realities, and much more than we could imagine. For example, imagine the big bang starting differently repeatedly. We are only in one possibility of all those possibilities, and each possibility can have different courses of history. This is only my imaginative taste. Assume there is a plurality of worlds just as real as our world. In which way is that consideration useful? I can say there is this world full of giraffes, that there is no gravity, and that everything is purple. So now what? I opened that possibility. What could I do with it? A video game? A cartoon? Lewis does not care about what we are capable of imagining. He simply defined a system and its structure; he justified modality. He concluded with an inflated ontology. Is it worth it? Are there really other possible worlds? In the end, we do not know. This is an *argumentum ad ignorantiam*, meaning lack of contrary evidence, which is a logical fallacy, and that is how metaphysics work, until it becomes physics. Lewis' theory is designed so that it stays within the metaphysical range. It cannot be proved correct, but neither can it be proved false. It is, by all means, unscientific. What makes it unfalsifiable, I believe, is that knowledge moves forward from the logical to metaphysical range, which in turn moves forward to the physical range. Although the many-worlds interpretation of quantum mechanics cannot be compared with genuine modal realism because physicists assume that we could prove their existence, Lewis claims they are definitionally, causally isolated.[32] Disparate conceptions of worlds are possible, and despite challenging common sense and violation of the law of parsimony, I believe in different conceptions. This implies that pos-

---

[32]Were this true, it would be impossible to travel to other Lewisian worlds, but it would be possible to travel to other Everettian worlds.

sible worlds reference different entities, some ersatz worlds exist in logical space as abstract representations, Lewisian worlds belong to metaphysical space, and Everettian worlds are part of our physical reality. It is difficult to see everything radically from a single viewpoint; it blinds possibilities and neglects many questions. Many issues remain unresolved. I inquire about counterparts and double lives. I do not see it necessary that it has to be either counterparts or double lives. Both could be true. I feel a false dichotomy. Evidently, reality would be much more complex. Sometimes it is easy to understand what possible worlds are, and then it goes away, but it returns and repeats. I am certain that this will remain a mystery during my life, and in the meantime, humanity will make use of intellectual tools.

Conclusion

Ersatz possible worlds are useful for representing impossibilities and objects that do not exist. But, we do not achieve the desired reduction, which is crucial for gaining modal knowledge. I am against extended modal realism, nevertheless, I consider that impossibilities can be represented by ersatz possible worlds. Our epistemic access seems to be a representation of possible worlds, which is in contrast to our actual world where we have direct access to concrete objects, because we are here; we have an indirect access to possible worlds through language. I consider myself a hybrid modal realist, it is possible that Lewisian worlds exist. It is a good theory that says that they exist. Lewisian worlds cannot be ruled out, even if we cannot prove them. Many issues remain unresolved. I inquire about counterparts and double lives. I do not see it necessary that it has to be either counterparts or double lives. Both could be true. I feel a false dichotomy. Evidently, reality would be much more complex. A plurality of worlds would exist, and these possible worlds would have parallel realities.

My conclusion is rationalist since abstractionism is based on reason. Modal realism demonstrates the rational power of human beings. It is a tool that exposes the power of rational thinking. The concept of possible worlds is a great philosophical tool. Just like numbers, there exist myriad applications. One use is to apply intellectual tools, but another is to reflect on their existence. Scientists use definitions, but philosophers raise doubts about established concepts, and inquire about definitions.

Bibliography

Adams, Robert M. (1974). "Theories of Actuality". In: *Noûs* 8.3, pp. 211–231.

Armstrong, David M. (1989). *A Combinatorial Theory of Possibility*. Ed. by Sydney Shoemaker. New York: Cambridge studies in Philosophy.

Barwise, Jon (1997). "Information and Impossibilities". In: *Notre Dame Journal of Formal Logic* 38.4, pp. 488–515.

Berto, Francesco (2010). "Impossible Worlds and Propositions: Against the Parity Thesis". In: *The Philosophical Quarterly (1950-)* 60.240, pp. 471–486.

Blackburn, Simon (1984). *Spreading the Word: Groundings in the Philosophy of Language*. Clarendon Press.

Bricker, Phillip (2001). "Island Universes and the Analysis of Modality". In: *Reality and Humean Supervenience: Essays on the Philosophy of David Lewis*. Ed. by G. Preyer and F. Siebelt. Rowman and Littlefield.

Cameron, Ross P. (2007). "The Contingency of Composition". In: *Philosophical Studies: An International Journal for Philosophy in the Analytic Tradition* 136.1, pp. 99–121.

Cocchiarella, Nino B. and Max A. Freund (2008). *Modal Logic. An Introduction to Its Syntax and Semantics*. New York: Oxford University Press.

Cresswell, Max J. (1979). *The Possible and the Actual. Readings in the Metaphysics of Modality*. Ed. by Michael J. Loux. New York: Cornell University Press.

Divers, John (2002). *Possible Worlds*. New York: Routledge.

Garson, James (2016). "Modal Logic". In: *The Stanford Encyclopedia of Philosophy*. Ed. by Edward N. Zalta. Spring 2016.

Girle, Rod (2009). *Modal logics and philosophy*. 2. Durham: Acumen.

Hume, David (1793). *Essays, moral, political and literary*. Essays and Treatises on Several Subjects. T. Cadell, London.

Kant, Immanuel (2003). *Critique of Pure Reason*. Translated by J. M. D. Meiklejohn. New York: Dover Philosophical Classics.

King, Peter J. (1995). "Other Times". In: *Australasian Journal of Philosophy* 73.4.

Kment, Boris (2012). "Varieties of Modality". In: *The Stanford Encyclopedia of Philosophy*. Ed. by Edward N. Zalta. Winter 2012.

Kripke, Saul A. (1988). *Naming and Necessity*. Malden: Black.

Laan, David A. Vander (1997). "The Ontology of Impossible Worlds". In: *Notre Dame Journal of Formal Logic* 38.4, pp. 597–620.

Lewis, David K. (1968). "Counterpart Theory and Quantified Modal Logic". In: *The Journal of Philosophy* 65.5, pp. 113–126.

— (1973). "Causation". In: *The Journal of Philosophy* 70.17, pp. 556–567.

— (1986). *On the Plurality of Worlds*. Malden: Blackwell Publishing.

Look, Brandon C. (2013). "Leibniz's Modal Metaphysics". In: *The Stanford Encyclopedia of Philosophy*. Ed. by Edward N. Zalta. Spring 2013.

Loux, Michael J., ed. (1979). *The Possible and the Actual. Readings in the Metaphysics of Modality*. New York: Cornell University Press.

Lycan, William (1979). *The Possible and the Actual. Readings in the Metaphysics of Modality*. Ed. by Michael J. Loux. New York: Cornell University Press.

Meinong, Alexius (1960). *Realism and the Background of Phenomenology*. Ed. by Roderick M. Chisholm. Illinois: The Free Press of Glencoe.

Menzel, Christopher (2016). "Possible Worlds". In: *The Stanford Encyclopedia of Philosophy*. Ed. by Edward N. Zalta. Spring 2016.

Miller, Alexander (2014). "Realism". In: *The Stanford Encyclopedia of Philosophy*. Ed. by Edward N. Zalta. Winter 2014.

Nolan, Daniel (1996). "Recombination Unbound". In: *Philosophical Studies: An International Journal for Philosophy in the Analytic Tradition* 84.2/3, pp. 239–262.

— (2005). *David Lewis*. Ed. by John Shand. Philosophy now.

— (2016). "Modal Fictionalism". In: *The Stanford Encyclopedia of Philosophy*. Ed. by Edward N. Zalta. Spring 2016.

Parsons, Terence (1982). "Are There Nonexistent Objects?" In: *American Philosophical Quarterly* 19.4, pp. 365–371.

Plantinga, Alvin (1969). "De Re et De Dicto". In: *Noûs* 3.3, pp. 235–258.

— (1976). "Actualism and possible worlds". In: 42, pp. 139–160.

— (1987). "Two Concepts of Modality: Modal Realism and Modal Reductionism". In: *Philosophical Perspectives* 1, pp. 189–231.

Priest, Graham (1997). "Sylvan's Box: A Short Story and Ten Morals". In: *Notre Dame Journal of Formal Logic* 38.4, pp. 573–582.

— (2005). *Towards Non-being the Logic and Metaphysics of Intentionality*. Oxford: Clarendon Press.

— (2008). *An Introduction to Non-Classical Logic. From If to Is*. 2. New York: Cambridge Introductions to Philosophy.

Quine, Willard V. (1948). "On What There Is". In: *The Review of Metaphysics* 2.5, pp. 21–38.

— (1968). "Propositional Objects". In: *Crítica: Revista Hispanoamericana de Filosofía* 2.5, pp. 3–29.

Ramírez, Eduardo García (2015). *Sobre la Pluralidad de Mundos*. By David K. Lewis. Distrito Federal: Universidad Nacional Autónoma de México.

Reicher, Maria (2015). "Nonexistent Objects". In: *The Stanford Encyclopedia of Philosophy*. Ed. by Edward N. Zalta. Winter 2015.

Restall, Greg (1997). "Ways Things Can't Be". In: *Notre Dame Journal of Formal Logic* 38.4, pp. 583–597.

Rosen, Gideon (1995). "Modal Fictionalism Fixed". In: *Analysis* 55.2, pp. 67–73.

Rosenberg, Alexander (1989). "Is Lewis's 'Genuine Modal Realism' Magical Too?" In: *Mind* 98.391, pp. 411–421.

Russell, Bertrand A. (1905). "On Denoting". In: *Mind* 14.56, pp. 479–493.

Rynasiewicz, Robert (2014). "Newton's Views on Space, Time, and Motion". In: *The Stanford Encyclopedia of Philosophy*. Ed. by Edward N. Zalta. Summer 2014.

Shalkowski, S. A. (2014). "The Ontological Ground of the Alethic Modality". In: *The Philosophical Review* 103.4, pp. 669–688.

Sider, Theodore (2003). "Reductive Theories of Modality". In: *The Oxford Handbook of Metaphysics*. Ed. by M. J. Loux and D.W. Zimmerman, pp. 180–208.

Skow, Bradford (2008). "Haecceitism, Anti-Haecceitism and Possible Worlds". In: *The Philosophical Quarterly (1950-)* 58.230, pp. 98–107.

Skyrms, Brian (1981). "Tractarian Nominalism (For Wilfrid Sellars)". In: *Philosophical Studies: An International Journal for Philosophy in the Analytic Tradition* 40.2, pp. 199–206.

Spade, Paul Vincent and Claude Panaccio (2015). "William of Ockham". In: *The Stanford Encyclopedia of Philosophy*. Ed. by Edward N. Zalta. Fall 2015.

Stalnaker, Robert C. (1976). "Possible Worlds". In: *Noûs* 10.1, pp. 65–75.

— (1996). "Impossibilities". In: *Philosophical Topics* 24.1, pp. 193–204.

Uzquiano, Gabriel (2015). "Recombination and Paradox". In: *Philosophers Imprint* 15.19, pp. 1–20.

Vaidya, Anand (2015). "The Epistemology of Modality". In: *The Stanford Encyclopedia of Philosophy*. Ed. by Edward N. Zalta. Summer 2015.

Yagisawa, Takashi (1988). "Beyond Possible Worlds". In: *Philosophical Studies: An International Journal for Philosophy in the Analytic Tradition* 53.2, pp. 175–204.

Zalta, Edward N. (2011). "Logic and Metaphysics". In: *Logic and Philosophy Today*, pp. 153–182.

Index